Wishing you both great adventures. I will miss you guys! Heather xo

Good luck and
Don't forget us
Best of luck in everything
you do
Debbie

Good Luck -
Dick & Kathy
Specht

Best of Luck!
Glad to have met
you!
Russ

Joel R Specht

Have Fun
Live Laugh Love
Have a great time!! :)
Sue
P.S. Pine-nutty
927 Main St
44030

Wishing you a
wonderful future!
Naomi

Good Luck
&
Don't forget us!
♥ Darlene

You'll have to come
back in Januaries to
visit & remember the wonderful
snow belt. Oh yeah - and to
see us :)!
Kenna

It is simple to be difficult.
It is difficult to be simple.
But it is simply difficult to be
Beautiful...

Let's try to be Beautiful

Magical Mosaic Of Ashtabula County

Photography,
Graphics , Designing
Editing And Publishing
by:
Parminder Singh M.D.

Poetry by:
Claudia Greenwood

Text by:
Frank Obernyer

Captions by:
Martha Stump Benson

Printed in China
Published in 2002

Library of Congress Control #
2002090412

ISBN: 0-9704318-2-1

10 9 8 7 6 5 4 3 2

Published in the United States of America by
Parminder Singh M.D.
235 B Parrish Rd.
Conneaut, Ohio, 44030
(440)-593-6319
parminsd@yahoo.com

Cover: Cederquist Park, Ashtabula

Back Cover: Beautiful County

Right: Ashtabula Lighthouse (1905)

Dedicated to my children

Open to the world,
ports of Ashtabula County
extend her horizon
beyond imagining.

Old Coast Guard Station at Ashtabula Harbor

Ashtabula is but mid-way
in a long journey which begins at the point
of a miner's pick deep in the Appalachian hills.
Dominating the harbor,
the over-arching coal conveyer transports
Ohio's black gold
from upended rail cars
into cavernous holds of lake freighters.

Above: Winter Scene-Ashtabula River.

Contents

ASHTABULA COUNTY

In the Middle — First Step Beyond the Colonies

Ashtabula County, the first step beyond the original thirteen colonies, evolved from a history and heritage tempered by the taming of the wilderness begun by New England settlers more than 200 years ago.

This is the story of the beauty of the land, climate and people as seen through the eyes of those who settled here and of those who live here today. Local geography, sculpted by glaciers and worked by man, immensely impacted both the minds and spirits of those who chose to call this land home.

Through the lens and eyes of Dr. Parminder Singh, yesteryear's wild, untamed beauty is seen again as if for the first time. Beauty, natural and man-made, surrounds our daily lives but often goes unnoticed in its fleeting passage.

Evolution results from constant, never ending change. In that change, and in our perception of it, lies the magic. Our perception of the realities of the past, present and future makes us what we are today.

This collection of magical images captures the beauty found in space and time, and presents a colorful, rich account of what we have, who we are, and how we evolved. This magical mosaic serves simultaneously as a record of change, perseverance and preservation.

Like our cherished covered bridges, the ensuing mosaic spans centuries, revealing the form, function and beauty of our achievements while leaving us with a sense of awe of who we were and who we've become.

Welcome to Ashtabula County!

The Magical Land

Dense virgin forest stretched far beyond what the human eye could behold. It was said a squirrel could climb a tree on the southern shore of Lake Erie, and travel branch-to-branch to the Ohio River without ever touching the ground. Hilly terrain, replete with mature hardwoods, was home to wild river gorges and vast tracts of wetlands and swamp.

The land teemed with white-tailed deer, beaver, mink, and fox; was also home to black bear, gray wolf, panther, lynx, wild boar, and swamp rattlesnake. Then, as today, squirrel, raccoon, opossum, woodchuck and rabbit were commonplace.

By 1830, beaver were nowhere to be found in Ohio. Deer disappeared from the landscape for more than fifty years, and the carrier pigeon became extinct. In the early 19th century, immense flocks of carrier pigeons would darken the midday sun as they rose in flight from their forest roosts.

Today, as in pre-settler times, deer and beaver once again are plentiful, thanks to recent preservation and conservation efforts. The swamp rattlesnakes can still be found in local wetlands, but present and future generations will never experience the midday eclipse caused by the carrier pigeon.

The yellow poplar, cucumber tree and red cedar, to name a few, were indigenous to the Ohio forest. Flowering dogwood, wild plum, cherry and crab apple were commonplace, as were the native gooseberry and willow bushes.

Swamps were home to popular trees and cottonwoods, and to swamp rattlers, which were the only poisonous snakes native to what was to become Ashtabula County. The reptile was so plentiful, young men would hunt them for sport, often killing dozens in only a few hours.

Peat bogs, living relics of the Ice Age, dotted the landscape and provided habitat for songbirds, reptiles, amphibians and insects. Needle-shedding tamaracks, blueberries, ferns and cotton grass thrived in or near yellow-green carpets of sphagnum moss, which were decorated with flowering orchids, most notable being the dragon's mouth and the lady's slipper.

The Western Reserve's bog habitats exist in all stages of evolution, dating from the last retreat of mile-high glaciers to the present day. The last glacial advance scraped hilltops, filled valleys with rock, soil and debris. Its retreat and consequent meltdown left behind seeds and spores from more northern and colder climates.

Species which migrated southward with the glacier thrived in the woodland swamps of Northeast Ohio – especially in the great Pymatuning Swamp. Mutations adapted to the warmer climes. Many of these unique fauna, however, have disappeared under the manmade lake, and from the vanishing wetlands which are drained for present and future development.

Many plants are now extinct, but occasionally, as in 1978, a species thought to have vanished is rediscovered. The native Canadian St. John's wort was sighted near Orwell in a wetland area. In ancient times, the wort was burned to ward off witches, goblins and devils.

During the glacial age, the Ashtabula and Grand rivers, as well as Indian and Conneaut creeks, all flowed southward. The north and south ridges of the county, once beachheads of Lake Erie, resulted from glacial action. The mouth of the "Geaugah" (Grand) River at Lake Erie was diverted westward from Geneva to Fairport.

***

The Indian Nations

The great forest's hardwood timbers were revered by the confederated tribes of both the Iroquois and Algonquian nations. The "Hash-tah-buh-lah" River, so named by the Algonquians and translated as "fish river" or "river of many fish," served as the international boundary separating the territories of the two nations.

The Iroquois Nation, consisting of the Mohawk, Oneida, Onondaga, Cayuga and Seneca tribes, ruled the wilderness from the Ashtabula River eastward into Pennsylvania and western New York.

They were the victors in the bloody Beaver Wars of the 1650's, wars of genocide resulting in the near extinction of the Nation of the Cat (raccoon), the Erie tribe after whom the lake was named. Few, if any Eries, once numbering more than 16,000, were ever seen by white settlers.

The Eries, warring lovers of freedom, fell victim to what may have been the first arms race of the New World, for the Iroquois had gained advantage with the purchase of guns from the early Dutch traders, and later from the French as middlemen in the fur trade.

The shrewd Iroquois knew that as long as they controlled the fur trade with the French, they would also win the arms race with neighboring tribal rivals. As the Ohio and New York fur trade trapped out, the Iroquois set their sights westward. They warred without mercy on the Hurons, Tobacco Nation, Wyandots, and Eries, in their quest for control of the western Great Lakes fur trade.

Remains of two Indian forts, built for defense by the Eries, are to be found today in Wayne Township and at Warner's Hollow in Windsor Township. Other earthen-work fortifications, located deep within the Pymatuning Swamp, were lost with the creation of the modern lake with the same name.

The major battle between the Iroquois and the Eries is thought to have taken place along Conneaut ("where snows remain late") Creek. The poison arrows of the Eries kept the gun-bearing invaders at bay until the Iroquois used their canoes as shields as they stormed the earthwork defenses.

Warriors, women and children were all killed. No prisoners were taken, and few escaped the wrath of the Iroquois. It was said that blood ran knee-deep within the earthworks on that fateful day.

This battle, in the mid-17th century, was the last warring encounter to occur in what is now Ashtabula County. The first settlers were to benefit, for there were no warring tribes here to interfere with their efforts to tame the Ohio wilderness and build new homes.

The Cat Nation's way of life and survival depended on plantings of squash, maize and beans; harvesting and processing of maple syrup; gathering of nuts and berries; hunting of deer, bear and fowl; and fishing. Similar subsistence diets served early white settlers in the years immediately following the American Revolution and the War of 1812.

The Algonquian Nation was a confederation of the Lenape (Delaware), Miami, Ottawa, Shawnee, Chippewa and Wyandot tribes. The Delaware, believed to be the original Algonquian tribe, previously were driven by early colonists from their homeland along the Delaware River near the Atlantic coastline. The Lenape (true men) were the Indians who sold Manhattan Island to the Dutch in 1626. By 1750, they had migrated to Ohio to escape from the onslaught of white settlement along the Atlantic seaboard. This would be the first of six major migrations to the Northeastern corner of Ohio within the last three centuries.

Though many westward-fleeing Delaware were conquered by the Iroquois, those who made it to Ohio became powerful and maintained their independence. Friendly with the French traders and missionaries, the Delaware fought against the British during the French and Indian War, and later sided with the American colonists in their War of Rebellion.

The Delaware remained independent and waged war on early settlers in western Ohio and in Indiana until they surrendered their lands at the Treaty of Greenville, following General Anthony Wayne's victory at the Battle of Fallen Timbers in 1796. From that time until the War of 1812, there were no Indian raiding parties active in Northern Ohio.

Few Indians remained in the eastern half of the Western Reserve at the time of its early settlement by New Englanders. Chippewa Indians continued to make their yearly journey by canoe from the western shores of Lake Michigan to the Ashtabula County area. Here they hunted bountiful game in the southern townships, gathered salt from the licks near present day Poland, and made maple sugar from the forest maples.

Omic, the Beaver, was the last ruling chief of the Algonquians to live in Ashtabula County. He befriended many of the early settlers of the county.

John Babcock, a noted pioneer hunter who settled northwest of Orwell, was rumored to have killed the last Indian warrior in an incident which supposedly took place along Rock Creek in Orwell Township in 1818 or 1819.

The last Indians reported here were Senecas, seen hunting and fishing along Mills Creek in Denmark Township as late as 1821. In 1829, the federal government moved the Delaware tribe from their Ohio reservation onto reservations in Kansas and Oklahoma.

The Ohio Wilderness, once the bountiful hunting ground for all the Great Lakes tribes, was ripe and ready for picking, as the War of Rebellion was won by George Washington, and the confederation of colonies was formed. The Western Reserve, freed of all former alliances and treaties, was waiting for settlers and civilization.

Treaties between the English and Indian tribes regarding the western Ohio territories were no longer valid. Washington had his own vision, and moved quickly to ensure colony control over the coveted frontier lands beyond the Appalacian Mountains.

***

Late day suncolors
spill onto the river,
their weight pressing down,
stopping it, still.

Dried leaves,
cupped vessels,
approach then cross
the ever-so-slightly shimmering
reflections of the trees,
betraying the deep current,
the constant motion
of the river
that appears to have stopped,
so still.

Reflecting the beauty of fall, Conneaut Creek winds its way through peak foliage west of Middle Road Covered Bridge.

Above & Next Page:

Wonders of the snow in the County.

Silently,
miraculous flakes fall,
one atop another.
Weighing nothing separately,
but bending great branches
in their collaborative effort,
they alter a landscape overnight.

The Ancients

The Algonquians and Iroquois, however, were not the first to live in the Ohio lands later known as the Western Reserve. They were preceded by mound builders, who left burial mounds in Wayne and Rome townships, and in Ashtabula.

The mound builders, in turn, were preceded by a race of giants (Massanga), whose cemeteries were discovered in both Conneaut and Ashtabula. The four-acre burial ground in Conneaut holds the graves of more than 2,000. Ashtabula's east side burial ground had a population of more than 1,000.

A manuscript, reportedly found in 1809 in a cave along "Conneaught" (Conneaut) Creek by a Rev. Solomon Spaulding, is believed by some to be the basis for the Book of Mormon. Interpretations of the document indicate the race of giants could have been the Jaredites, the long lost tribe of Israel.

A second early document, now in the archives at Oberlin College, tells of the Roman general, Fabius, whose ship was blown westward to the land of the Deleware. Supposedly, he was bound for the British Isles when his ship encountered stormy weather and was windblown to the shores of the New World.

Whether or not these documents existed and were discovered in Ashtabula County does not alter historical facts regarding who made claim to the lands where we now live. All who lived here – giants, mound builders, redmen, trappers, missionaries, explorers and early settlers – followed the streams and lakes as they traversed this beautiful, untamed land.

The most traveled trade route was the Watershed Trail, which could be traveled by canoe with minimal portage from the Atlantic Ocean to the Gulf of Mexico. This easternmost trade route divide of the north and south watersheds is located in the Dorset swamp.

The swamp serves as headwaters for both Mills Creek and Pymatuning Creek. Mills Creek runs north and west to the Grand River, which dumps into Lake Erie and beyond to the Atlantic. Pymatuning ("Whispering Waters") Creek runs southward to the Ohio and Mississippi rivers and on into the Gulf. Only a short portage separates these two headwaters, and those who preceded us made frequent use of this transportation waterway.

Flint artifacts, found in the county, are indiginous with Rocky Mountain flint, proving the local Indian populations traveled and traded across the length and breadth of the continent. Transportation, by foot and by water, was as necessary for survival then as modern modes of transportation are today.

Mastadon bones were discovered in 1878 at Boudinot Seely's farm near Center Creek in Austinburg, and today remain in the care of the Natural History Museum in Cleveland. The mastadon roamed the woodland environment of northern Ohio in the Paleolithic Era more than 10,000 years ago.

The ancients would run the ten-foot tall, five-ton beasts into the swamps. When the mastadon bogged down in the mire, the ancient hunters would move in for the kill with flint and stone-headed spears.

Perhaps the first non-Indian to view the Ohio Wilderness along the southern shore of Lake Erie was a trapper, explorer and adventurer named Etienne Stephen Brule. Brule lived with the Hurons in the early 17th century on the northern lake shore.

He also lived for a short time with the Senecas, but returned to the Hurons, whose lifestyle was more to his liking. Brule, first came to the New World as a teenage adventurer with the French explorer Champlain. When Champlain took a native Huron to France, Brule was left behind in the native's place.

Was Brule merely insurance for the safe return of the traveling native, or was he a willing partner in the New World's first student exchange program?

It's unfortunate that little is known about the ancient people who lived here prior to the reign of the two nations which Brule knew and adopted. Our early history paints the Indian as savage and gives little credit to his civilized way of life. By discrediting the Indian as being savage, it was easier for the white man to justify genocide and to take control of the land claimed by the tribes.

***

Connecticut's Western Reserve

Winning of the West began in Ohio. However, before the first settler arrived, many battles were fought regarding claims to 4,764,600 acres, later known as the Western Reserve. Once surveyed, however, the Reserve proved to contain only 3,667,000 acres.

Claims to lands located west of the Appalacian Mountains were held simultaneously by England, France, Virginia, Massachusetts, Connecticut and several Indian tribes. France lost her claim as a result of the French and Indian War, while England lost her claim when she lost the War of Rebellion with her colonies.

With England's loss also went the claims of the Indians, for their treaties with the British were not recognized by the new American government. Washington's government was given the tasks of negotiating new treaties with the Indian tribes and of settling the conflicting land claims of the three states. Connecticut had additional land-claim disputes with New York and Pennsylvania, which complicated any final agreement.

Above & Left:
The peace and serenity of Lake Erie
at Sun Set Park, North Kingsville.

We come to the end of each day
safe in the assumption
that the colors of closure
which slip beyond the horizon
will be enriched overnight
to return,
brush strokes of renewed energy
at dawn.

The gumdrop world
reflected in the water
is sweet and tempting.
It is also transient.

Losing their grasp of summer,
leaves, brilliant spinnakers unfurled,
will enter the parade down river
toward winter.

In but a few days
great maples and oaks
will stand, quite naked, on the bank,
the parade having passed them by.

Previous Page:

Pond reflection near
Creek Road Covered Bridge.

Left:

Water fall near
Creek Road Covered Bridge.

Below:

Pond On Stevens Road

Healing begins when
we pause at the edge
of a woodland pond
and join the forest green.

Connecticut had received its charter from King Charles II in 1662, and was deeded land "sea-to-sea" for a 62-mile wide strip. Pennsylvania's charter, also from Charles II, was secured some 20 years later than Connecticut's, and included land already deeded to Connecticut.

The oversight on the King's part was not a problem until Connecticut ran short of farmland for its growing population. Yankees, as Connecticut residents were called, moved into the yet unsettled Wyoming Valley in northwestern Pennsylvania to establish claim to lands they believed were theirs according to the "sea-to-sea" clause of their charter.

The Yankee nickname was an insult to the Connecticut New Englanders because it referred to their sharp trading practices. The term "yankee" was equal to being called a pirate, after the Dutch pirate "Janke".

Pennsylvanians, whom the Yankees referred to as Pennamites, disagreed, and the Yankee-Pennamite Wars resulted. The new federal government resolved the land-claim issues by taking title to all lands of the Northwest Territory except those of Connecticut's Western Reserve.

Connecticut retained its reserve as compensation for lands lost in the inter-state settlement. The Nutmeg state immediately sold their Western Reserve for the sum of $1,200,000 to 52 speculators who formed the Connecticut Land Company in 1795.

Clear title, however, was not forthcoming from the federal government until 1800. Connecticut used the proceeds from the sale to fund the educational needs of their state. To this date, the original $1.2 million endowment of the Connecticut Education Fund has yet to be touched.

Early Settlement

"The pioneers who first broke ground here accomplished a work unlike that which will fall to the lot of any succeeding generation. The hardships they endured, the obstacles they encountered, the life they led, the peculiar qualities they needed in their undertakings and the traits of character developed by their work, stand alone in our history. These pioneers knew well that the three forces, which constitute the strength and glory of a free government, are the family, the school and the church." James A. Garfield

There were as many reasons for coming to the western wilderness of Ohio as there were settlers who made the long and difficult journey, mostly from Connecticut, Massachusetts and New York.

Promises of cheap land, financial opportunity, religion, adventure and glory headed the list of motivations for the early migration during the historical period of the formation of the new nation.

Immediately following the War of Rebellion, life in Connecticut was not what it used to be under British rule. The land was wearing out, and harvests were down; farms were in disrepair, showing neglect and abuse suffered during the war; taxes were no longer due the king, but the church was taking double the king's former share.

Those who came brought along their industrious Puritan heritage from their Connecticut homeland. The result was the establishment of a distinctive atmosphere and style of living – a culture unique in all of Ohio.

Once in the Western Reserve, settlers were first molded by Indians who walked the southern shores of Lake Erie. Early settlers depended on friendly Indians for survival – for food, trade, guidance and information.

They cleared the land and became dirt farmers. They hunted the forests and became riflemen. They built the first mills and became mechanics. They constructed unique buildings and became artisans. They worked together building communities and became leaders of government and business. Most of all, they adapted to the new land.

Some came westward with new spouses, escaping from unhappy and untenable domestic situations in New England; some came for land ownership, a first-time experience for descendents of Connecticut's labor force – the indentured servant; some came to escape from the suffocating confines of their Puritan religion.

There were no roads to Ohio. The first pioneers brought along what supplies and possessions they could. They endured inclement weather, mud, swarming insects, sickness and cold, and thieves to get to Ohio.

Cont. Page 30

Conneaut Lighthouse

Who can say
what paths we'll take
when so many stretch before us?
Who can know
before the step
where the next will lead?
Who but those who stand
in the center
reflecting on the
choices
the changes
        the twists
                the turns
the Way...
        the ways,
                the Light.

Page 24, 25:

A tranquil fall day at Lakeshore Park in Ashtabula. For almost a century, area residents and others have enjoyed the benefits of this popular park.

Late summer sun
boils the sap
of the towering maples.
It evaporates
into the close,
dense air,
a potent elixir
for the overwhelming
melancholy
that comes with the
first brush strokes of color
on treetops across the county,
the gathering of migratory birds,
the sudden awareness
of the passing
of summer.

Harpersfield with autumn splendor.

Conneaut Creek near Creek Rd. Covered Bridge.

Next Page:

Columns of ice are a familiar and fascinating winter scene along the steep shale banks bordering our many streams and creeks.

In any season but winter
such miracles of nature
as entwined branches,
complex geometric shapes,
simply engineered bridges
would go unnoticed.

Must it take such extreme conditions
for us to pay attention?

Cont. from Page 22..

Once here, the first order of business was to clear land for crops and a cabin site. Trees were felled and seeds were planted at once to ensure a first crop before winter. Often, trees were girded – a ring of bark was removed so sap would bleed from the tree depriving leaves of food. Once the leaves died and fell, planted crops received the necessary sunlight needed for growth.

Family members lived in crude lean-to shelters until a simple one-room cabin with a dirt floor could be raised. Fires were built on the floor, and smoke escaped through a hole in the roof. Most cooking, however, was done outside over an open fire. Standard fare was cornmeal mush and whatever game, if any, was brought home from the daily hunt.

James and Eunice Kingsbury arrived at Stow's Castle at Port Independence along Conneaut Creek in 1796. Kingsbury is credited with harvesting the first wheat in the Reserve. His son, Albert, was the first white child to be born in Ashtabula County. The child died of starvation that first winter. The Kingsburys moved to Cleveland in 1797, where they prospered as a family and in the community.

Stowe's Castle was built as the commissary for General Moses Cleaveland's party of fifty or more who were sent by the Connecticut Land Company to survey the Western Reserve so land could be lotteried to shareholders and then sold for settlement. This venture of speculation by the land company was the first real estate development in the western frontiers beyond the original 13 colonies.

Cleaveland's party arrived by boat at the mouth of Conneaut Creek on July 4, 1796. His survey teams battled mosquitos, gnats, rattlesnakes, wolves, bear, wildcats and boars. One team followed the Elliott Line at the Pennsylvania border southward. Sixty-eight miles and seventeen days later they marked the 41st parallel as the southeastern corner of the Western Reserve.

George Beckwith brought his family from the Austinburg, settlement founded by Judge Eliphalet Austin, to Ashtabula in 1803. He had no claim to the land where he built his cabin and is known by history as a squatter. During his first winter along the Ashtabula River, he walked to Austin's settlement for supplies to ward off starvation for his family.

His wife became alarmed when he failed to return. She locked her children in their cabin, and walked to Austinburg to find her husband. When she arrived, the Austin settlers helped her track her husband on his return trip to Ashtabula. They found him frozen to death in the January snow along the South Ridge "Girdled Road".

Mrs. Beckwith remained with her children in her cabin. She gave aid and shelter to new settlers who came to the Reserve, and was known to help travelers cross the Ashtabula River by hand-pulling a raft across by rope.

Colonel Alexander Harper founded the first permanent settlement in 1798 in what is now Harpersfield. The Harpers built Shandy Hall in Unionville in 1815, the oldest frame house in the Western Reserve, which today is a museum of the Western Reserve Historical Society.

Judge Eliphalet Austin founded his settlement in Austinburg in 1799. Matthew Hubbard, a land agent and surveyor for the Connecticut Land Company arrived in Ashtabula in 1804 and settled near the Beckwith cabin. The First United Church of Christ Congregational Church, founded by Reverened Joseph Badger, which still dominates the village green, was the first church built in the Western Reserve. The church dates to 1801 when it congregation numbered sixteen members.

Solomon Griswold settled in Windsor Township in 1798. Four years later, his daughter, Keziah, would open the county's first classroom in the local blacksmith's shop. The following year, in 1805, she taught ten children in the new log schoolhouse. In the same year, Windsor Corners boasted construction of its first frame house.

In 1800, Conneaut settlers Aaron Wright and Anna Montgomery walked 60 miles on foot through uncut virgin forest to Harpersfield to be married by the nearest justice of the peace. This was the first recorded marriage in what was to become Ashtabula County.

Travel from Connecticut to Ashtabula took 40 days by ox-drawn covered wagons. Hardships were not limited to poor road conditions and bad weather. There were also robbers to deal with, sickness, fleas at roadside inns, and bridgeless flooded streams to cross. Meals at the inns were often "hasty pudding," mush eaten by spoon out of one community bowl.

The second westward migration to Northeastern Ohio had begun. Connecticut landowners exchanged New England land for new land in the Reserve. Others were poor and in debt. They struggled to pay for their new farms and to survive. Some were adventurers who owned neither property nor money. They took up land and paid for it by working for others. The wealthy speculated and became proprietors with large land holdings.

The winning of the West had begun, and it began in Ohio. "The Yankee Exodus" would prove to be the most influential migration in United States history.

***

Root Rd. Covered Bridge.

Fresh snowfall
softens the light
and awakens the holiday spirit
in Conneaut.

A late evening sky silhouettes City Hall and the Harwood Block in Conneaut. Built in 1880, the Harwood Block is famous for the prefab front that was manufactured in Chicago.

Wayne Township is home to the grounds and annual show of Ashtabula County Antique Engine Club, (established, 1981). Held around the first week of July, the show draws crowds of ten thousand from many states across the country.

Left & Below:

Antique Cars Show in Conneaut

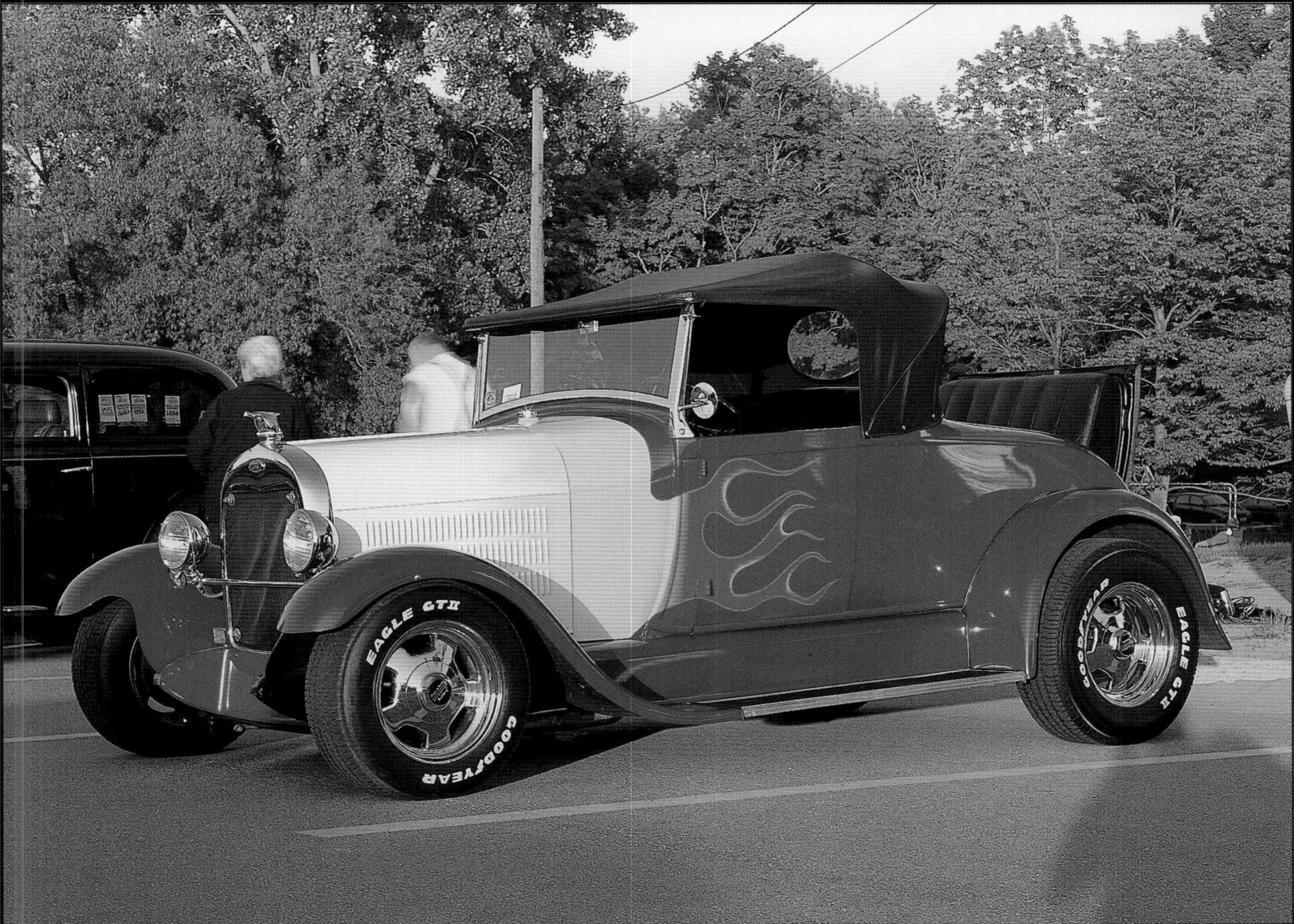

Commanding presences
in new, white robes,
these spruce trees
remind those of us who do
why we stay through winter
in Ashtabula County.

Parrish Road in Conneaut.

Survival in the Wilderness

"Much has been said of the hardships of the Puritan fathers – but Puritan mothers had to endure Puritan fathers". Frontier proverb.

Settlement of the Western Reserve was unique in the history of our country. Because land was purchased by parcel from land company speculators, early settlers were not afforded the luxury of the support of other settlers in a community. Each found his claim, cleared the land, built a cabin and survived as best he could alone, often twenty or more miles from his closest neighbor.

Goods were expensive and hard to come by. Those who were fortunate had oxen to help with the hard labor of clearing the land. Money was scarce and there were no markets for selling surplus goods. Whiskey was as good or better than legal tender. Transportation to eastern markets was expensive and time consuming.

Corn was the key for survival, as its uses were many. Mealfare often varied only with cornbread, johnnycakes, corndodgers, corn pone, cornmeal, parched corn and corn on the cob. The only relief depended upon what game was killed that day. Corn also provided fodder for bedding of livestock, insulation, kindling, mattress stuffing, toys and dolls, folk art, braided rugs, corncob pipes, and of course whiskey.

The Ohio pioneer women cooked over open fires; gathered food from forest, field and garden; carded, spun and wove wool and flax into cloth (linsey woolsy) to make clothing; bore children; practiced folk medicine to keep their families in good health; and guarded the livestock from preying wolves and bears. Women were also responsible for the moral and spiritual side of life.

Many women broke down and died under the burden of childbearing and hard toil. Children suffered whooping cough, scarlet fever, measles, dysentery and innumerable other maladies, and often died at a young age. Girls were expected to marry by age 16 or 17. All children worked the farm from the time they learned to walk.

The man was often gone from the homestead to purchase or barter for supplies. There were journeys to the salt licks and to the sugar groves. Whatever could be harvested and transported for value was taken full advantage of to keep the struggling family alive.

Men walked to market surplus goods in settlements often hundreds of miles away. They carried surplus goods and return supplies on their backs, because the horses or oxen were needed on the homestead to be worked by the children for the clearing of additional farmland.

Women often had difficulty coping with isolation and loneliness. Many suffered from a lostness known as a "species of delerium." Mental illness and suicide among women was not uncommon.

Most women who came to the Reserve, however, had the courage to stay. Some stayed not because the country was so good, but because thought of the journey back east was so bad.

Survival in the wilderness of the Western Reserve depended on "helpmate" partnerships. Though many of those who came to the Reserve were educated, there were no schools for their children to attend, and family efforts to survive left little time for home education. The first generation of the Western Reserve went to the school of hard knocks; yet, through their parents, they retained a taste for education which they would later bestow on their children.

The tools of conquest were the frontiersman's axe and the long rifle. The pioneer who cleared ten acres of land for each of ten years, and who reinvested profits from sales of surplus grain and wood into building livestock herds of horses, hogs, sheep and cattle, would then have a successful and profitable farm.

By 1811, only one farm in the county was known to be self-sufficient – that of Gideon Leet, Esquire, which was located along the east bank of the Ashtabula River in the Fields Brook area.

***

Lamp post at the Center Road bridge.

Right:

Popular and historic Walnut Beach, located at the end of Lake Ave. in Ashtabula, appears deserted on this quiet winter day.

Below:

Waterfall, Cederquist Park.

Silent now,
the pavilion awaits
boisterous summer days.

Early Roads and Mills

In 1798, the Connecticut Land Company anted up $2,600 to transform the old Indian trail, which rambled along the south ridge, into a roadway 25 feet wide with bridges to be built over streams. The Girdled Road, so called because all timber was girdled to a width of 33 feet, connected Conneaut to Cleaveland (Cleveland) via Sheffield, Plymouth, Austinburg, Harpersfield, Trumbull, Thompson, Leroy and Concord. This road is known today as South Ridge Road or State Route 84.

The western end of the new road followed the route into Cleaveland on what was to become Euclid Avenue. The eastern terminus connected to the Genesee Trail, which joined the Mohawk Valley Road at Fort Schyler to the Genesee River , located in New York. This road was formerly known as the Lake Trail or the Iroquois Trail, and would serve as the northern route for New England migration to the Western Reserve.

The 360-mile journey from New England to Ohio was a most difficult one and would not become the more traveler-friendly "Pennsylvania System" until the 1820's and 1830's. By that time the journey could be made comfortably via a combination of railroad, canal boat, horse car and stagecoach.

The State Road, connecting Warren to Painesville as a primary mail route was in use in 1800, and the north ridge road (now State Route 20) served as the first east-west stagecoach route.

The Salt Springs Road, the first north-south road in the county, was surveyed and legally established in 1802. The road to the Poland, Ohio salt springs followed another old Indian Trail from the Grand River south to Parkman, Nelson, Southington, Champion and Warren.

Along the way, several east-west roads branched into the main road, all becoming known in each local community as the salt road. State Route 45 was one of these branches, and was so well traveled as to become known as the Old Turnpike.

An evening sun touches the horizon on Lake Erie, illuminating clouds above with brilliant color.

Astabula Countians
are blessed
when a celestial orb
drops in,
on occasion,
to create such a memorable scene.

The northeast corner of Ohio boasts 17 wineries with a half dozen more to open in the next couple of years. It is also home to the largest and most acclaimed vineyards in the Buckeye state. More than 65% of all the grapes in the state are grown in this area. And in recent wine judgings across the county fully, 75% of all the medals awarded come from grapes grown along the Grand River Valley and the south shore of Lake Erie in Lake and Ashtabula counties. The State Trade Association, the Ohio Wine Producers Association, which represents more than 70 wineries state wide is located in Austinburg. Because of the respect that the regional industry has developed nationally, several of our professional winemakers and winegrowers annually are invited to speak at grape and wine conferences across the country. Ashtabula County can truly be proud of the fact that is is often viewed as 'the Napa Valley of the Midwest.'

Rounding out summer
to ripeness,
miles of vines
heavy with fruit
promise
flavorful accompaniments
to family dinners
and celebrations
all year long.

In 1803, a petition was approved for a second north-south road to connect Conneaut with Kinsman Mills. Low areas were filled with logs, making this road the first "corduroy" road in the county. Corduroy roads were constructed with logs, and were the predecessor to the wooden plank roads which became more commonplace in the early 19th century.

Serving the first range of towns – Conneaut, Monroe, Pierpont, Richmond, Andover and Williamsfield,— the road remains today with only two changes to its original survey and is known as Stanhope-Kelloggsville Road. The Geneva to Windsor Road was surveyed and under construction in 1804.

Sawmills and gristmills sprang up around the county, dominating any falls or rapids which would provide water power. The first gristmill in the county was built in Windsor Mills in 1800. Prior to this time, all grain requiring grinding was carried to Elk Creek, Pennsylvania, which was located 16 miles east of Conneaut.

Powder mills were built in Conneaut Harbor, on Bunker Hill and in West Andover. Both Austinburg and Windsor were home to powder storage houses by 1806. Wayne had both a watch tower and a powder house.

The first sawmill was constructed on the Grand River in 1801 near Austinburg by Ambrose Humphrey. Another appeared in Harpersfield in 1803. Within the span of a few years, mills were constructed on streams throughout the county and served as a magnet for early community development, but also served in turn as the community nemesis.

Most mills had a lifespan of five-to- eight years at one task and then were retrofitted for a more profitable industry. Many burned down at least once, or were destroyed in a "freshot," a sudden flood or water torrent. Many a pioneer was crippled or killed in a mill accident.

Worst of all, stagnant mill ponds were the environmental pollution problem of the early 19th century: they bred mosquitos and became the source of disease. Many were to suffer and die from the "ague," malarial fevers and chills.

By 1810, bankruptcy and debtor's prison faced the majority of landowners in the Western Reserve. Also at stake was the security of Connecticut's school fund. Less than 50 percent of the original $1.2 million had been paid into the Nutmeg state's coffers.

To deal with the problem, the Connecticut state legislature created the position of Commissioner of the School Fund and appointed former congressman James Hillhouse as commissioner with absolute power to resolve the issue.

For the next fifteen years, Hillhouse was to make annual trips to the Reserve by horse-drawn sulky. He became acquainted with every single debtor in the Reserve and with each debtor's state of personal affairs. What he found was extreme financial hardship. Hillhouse avoided litigation, made no charge for counseling of debtors and refused to send debtors to prison.

Instead, he bought time for settlers until canals opened up trade routes and until banks were chartered. By 1825, Hillhouse had collected all moneys owed plus an additional half million dollars. He single-handedly brought solvency to the Western Reserve, and was referred to as "The Guardian Angel of the Reserve."

***

Below & next page:

Saint Frances Cabrini Parish (Mother Cabrini) began as a mission church of Saint Mary in 1952 with Father Orlando Rich, assistant pastor of Saint Mary, to serve the needs of people of Saint Frances Cabrini. It was in 1955 that Saint Frances Xavier Cabrini was formerly declared a parish of the Diocese of Youngstown. The Saint Frances Xavier Cabrini School was formed in 1959 and renamed Saint Frances Community School after the consolidation with Saint Mary in 1972.

Overarching branches glisten.

How long they have grown
ring by ring,
with their trunk,
reaching up, reaching out,
reaching across.
Touching.

A lesson, perhaps, for those who live
on opposite sides of the street.

Traveling through majestic snow-covered trees, a car heads west on Lake Road toward Ashtabula harbor area.

This gigantic clock replica, located on the corner of Main and Broadway in Geneva, was manufactured in Cincinnati and purchased for the city around 1996.

Next page:

Christmas decorations brighten up a winter evening on South Broadway in Geneva.

Quiet Times and Prosperity

In 1803, when pioneers were first settling the Reserve, Ohio became a state. Much of the territory in the southeastern portion of the Ohio River basin had been settled prior to the settlement of the Western Reserve.

The Ohio Territory was established by the Northwest Ordinance of 1787. Together, with the Land Ordinance of 1785, the township was designated as the first form of local government. Ohio was designated as one county – Washington County. Soon after, using the Cuyahoga River as the dividing line, Washington County was split into two counties – Portage County to the west and Jefferson County to the east.

With federal settlement of western land claims, the Western Reserve was formed and soon after, in 1800, was given the county name of Trumbull, after Connecticut's governor. Warren became the county seat.

Salute to the Sun

Yoga practitioners all,
trees stand together,
branches outstretched,
reaching through time-worn wood
and supple leaf tips
toward the Light
that nourishes.

Ashtabula River

Previous Page:

Fall beauty, Hatches Corner Road.

It wasn't until 1807 that the county became known as Ashtabula County with its county seat to be located in Jefferson. Previously, Trumbull County was realigned and Ashtabula was in Geauga County with Chardon as its seat.

Gideon Granger, postmaster general for President Thomas Jefferson, founded Jefferson in 1804 but never lived there. He had a vision of his community becoming the political center of the county. He platted the village as a replica of Philadelphia, using the same street layout and street names.

Granger won the seat rights to the county in 1811 by beating out those who wanted the court house to be at an Eagleville site, which was then part of Austinburg. It cost him a generous donation of land and the construction of a jail and courthouse. At the time the first court house was constructed in 1815, Jefferson had only fifteen buildings to boast of along its muddy streets.

Prior to the formation of local government, the church served as the only court of law. Church fathers were often both judge and jury. Those accused, usually of adultery because they were not married, were excommunicated. Excommunication presented unbelievable hardships for the accused as they were cut off from all trade and friendship in their community.

Cont. Page 78

Winter at the Creamer Road.

Rare are the times
when ours are the first tracks.

So many go before us....

To see the world
from behind a shield
of icicles
is a rare opportunity indeed.
There must be languages
that don't even have the word
in their lexicon.

We must remember that fact
in January.

Icicles catch the red/gold of a sunrise on Parrish Road in Conneaut.

Kent State University, Ashtabula, is situated on 80 scenic acres overlooking Lake Erie. Built in 1966 and opened for classes in 1967, the campus serves the community by offering a variety of two-and four-year degree programs as well as graduate-level and non-credit continuing education courses. Collaboratively designed programs help local industry remain competitive in an ever-changing global economy.

Left:
Ashtabula River in fall beauty

A carpet of fall color surrounds the Sweet Park Gazebo. Located next to Wallace Braden School. The East Side Presbyterian Church can be seen in the background.

Fall in Conneaut.

Lake Erie

Conneaut Marina.

Downtown, Geneava.

St. Mary of the Immaculate Conception, Conneaut, established in 1847. The church building (back view) was dedicated in 1888 and the rear addition added at a later date. Located at the corner of State Route 20 and Chestnut St., the striking architecture of this beautiful church "draws the eye" of many as they pass by.

Left:

Waterfall, Rock Creek Park.

Next Page:

Rome Presbyterian Church (1836) in Rome Center was built along the lines of colonial architecture using native lumber and flagstones from Windsor quarry.

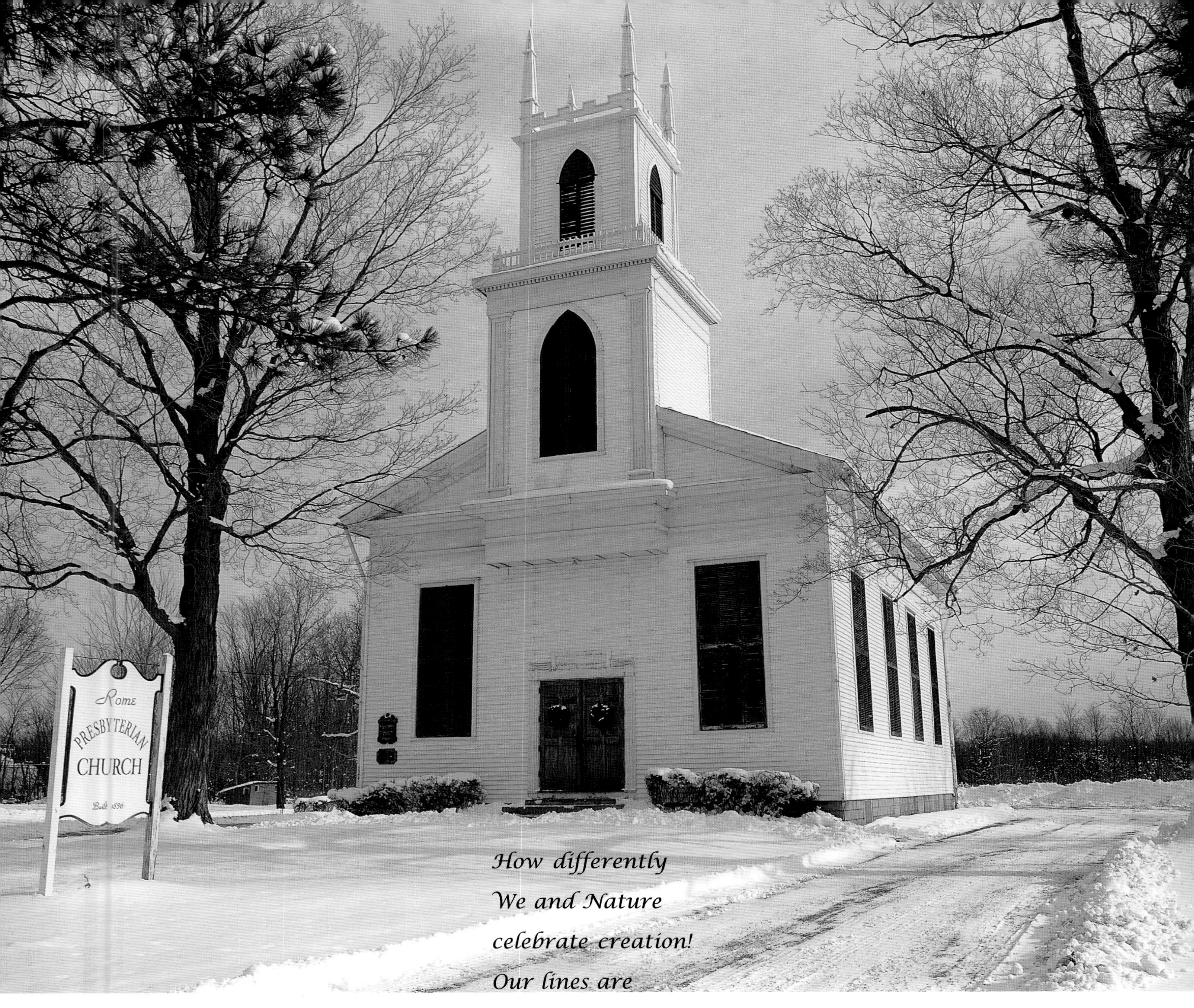

How differently
We and Nature
celebrate creation!
Our lines are
measured and precise.
Our structures,
bold and rigid.
Our utterances contained
within walls.

While Nature tumbles
over herself
with exuberance

or stretches awkwardly,
asymmetrically,
towards Heaven.

Below:

Ashtabula's war memorial with city hall in background.

Sunlight and shadows are reflected in this view of the Great lakes Marine and Coast Guard Museum at Ashtabula Harbor (Built in 1898).

Winter beauty.

Miniature Case Tractor

Case Steam Roller (1923) Used to roll sand for brick roads. Only 600 were made.

2378

The small community of ***Hartsgrove***, located at the corners of Rt. 534 and Rt. 6, is comprised of diversified buildings and businesses, including a general store, churches, gas stations, Masonic Lodge, Emporium & Presidential Museum, a gazebo in the park, and a country tavern known for "the best hamburgers around".

The natural dam and fresh water pond area behind Blakeslee log cabin was formed after construction of the nearby railroad and is home to a wide variety of fish and wildlife.

Near Blakslee Log Cabin.

Above & Next Page:

Adventure Zone, Geneva-On-The-Lake, was founded in 1997 to offer summer visitors as well as the residents of Ashtabula and neighboring counties a family oriented entertainment complex along the south shore of Lake Erie. Adventure Zone offers a full package of family fun in a safe, clean, and exciting environment: go karts, bumper boats, miniature golf, batting cages, a rock climbing and a repelling wall, snack foods, and various special activites on holiday weekends

Community Center, Dorset:

For almost a century, this former school building has served residents of the Dorset community. Since consolidation of the schools, a variety of activities have replaced the flow of students through its halls. The gymnasium of this 1913 school has hosted lodge and other meetings, receptions, dinners for up to 700 people, and even roller-skating. A log cabin served as the original school in 1823.

Left:

Main Street, Conneaut.

Next Page:

Bridge Street, Ashtabula Harbor.

MILLER ANDERSON CO
COLLECTIBLES NAUTICALS
CIRCA 1889
DIVINE COFFEE & TEA
LAW OFFICE

A winding, stony creek inspired the naming of **Rock Creek**. Once a thriving community, the town suffered many devastating fires from 1881 through 1924, losing most of the seventy businesses of that time. Rock Creek Rotary Park, with its twin falls and trails, is a popular spot for picnicking, hiking, swimming and fishing. The Rotary Club maintains the park.

Gazebo , Sweet Park
Ashtabula

Beautiful red leaves of
the Japanese Maple
cling to their branches
far into fall, often
catching the first fluffy
white snow for a
dramatic contrast.

Conneaut Marina.

Winter evening in Conneaut.

Next Page:

Ashtabula Harbor.

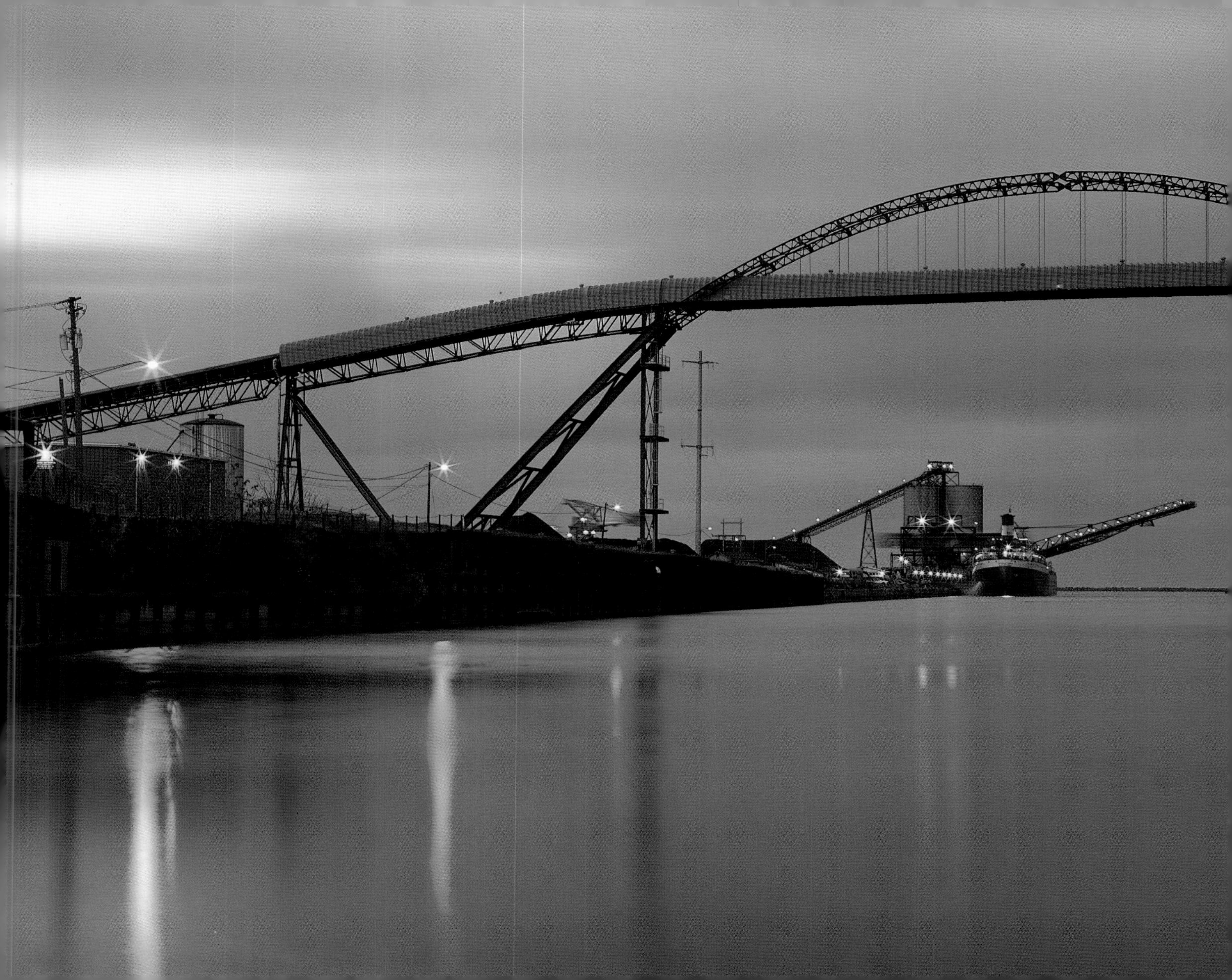

Cont. from Page 54..

These rigid practices were brought from the New England Puritan heritage. There were no known trials within Ashtabula County, but seven are on record in the Firelands, the western portion of the Western Reserve.

Migration to the Reserve increased in volume under second president John Adams. Harsh winters in Connecticut, resulting in crop failures spurred the movement. As county settlements grew, so did the need for schools and churches.

Traveling ministers, such as circuit-rider preacher Rev. Joseph Badger, were the norm, most preaching the Calvin version of Protestantism. Few churches were built prior to 1830. Early Protestant sects which thrived in the county were first the Congregationalists, followed by the Episcopalians, Presbyterians, and then by the Methodists and Baptists. It would not be until the 1850's before Jews and Catholics moved into the area in any great numbers.

The courthouse in Jefferson was opened every Sunday to permit preaching or religious meetings of any and all denominations. This practice continued until 1850.

One-room log schoolhouses sprung up and usually a young unmarried woman would be given the job of instilling the three "r's" into children of all grades. The only requirement for becoming a teacher was to be willing to teach and be able to maintain discipline.

Community members would take turn boarding the teacher, if she wasn't local, and she usually was paid with "trade" goods.

The Grand River Institute was chartered in 1831 as the Ashtabula County School of Science and Industry, and was located in Mechanicsburg. In 1835, the school and its buildings were moved to Austinburg, where it remains today and is known as the Grand River Academy.

The first election for county officials was held in 1807. Voting was so irregular, a somewhat unknown southern county candidate for commissioner complained to a visiting judge. The judge reviewed the election results, and threw out all votes counted in Jefferson, Austinburg, Harpersfield and Ashtabula because of ballot box stuffing.

PYMATUMING LAKE:

Over 50,000 years ago, a natural lake existed in this area. After the 10,000 year glacier meltdown, it evolved into a marsh covering some 23,000 acres and was known as the Great Pymatuming or Shanango swamp. Pymatuming Lake was formed with the building of a huge dam in the early 1930's. One-fourth of the shoreline borders the townships of Richmond, Andover and Williamsfield, attracting almost two million visitors a year for recreational activities.

The result was the four biggest names in the county – Granger, Austin, Harper and Hubbard – were excluded from office. Southern county influence was growing, and both north and south county were becoming aware of the other.

Joshua Reed Giddings, of Wayne Township, a young aspiring attorney opened his law office in Jefferson in 1823. He had recently completed his law studies under mentor Elisha Whittlesey in Canfield, a conservative federalist who served as a congressional legislator and later as a leading member of the Whig Party.

The first woolen mills were built prior to 1820, and early factories began to appear, producing chairs, castor oil, paper, cider, buttons, cheese and whiskey. In 1818, Captain Samuel Ward launched the "Salem Packet" from Conneaut Harbor, the first lake vessel of size to be built in the county.

This would be the start of the ship building industry in Conneaut, which soon would also bloom in Ashtabula. "The Tempest" was launched from Ashtabula in 1814, and in 1824 the State of Ohio passed legislation and funding to create a working harbor in that same city.

The Ashtabula Central Plank Road Company was busy constructing wooden plank roads, notably from Jefferson to Ashtabula and from Jefferson to Dorset. Tolls ranged from three-to-five cents.

Covered wooden bridges were constructed across the county's streams. These "kissin' bridges," the forerunners to the tunnels of love, provided the critical groundwork for the area's transportation system. The 154-foot Mechanicsville-Windsor Road Covered Bridge, first built in 1820, remains in service to local traffic today.

In today's modern era, road engineers continue to match wits with Mother Nature on how to best handle snow and ice on bridge surfaces. In contrast, during the 1800's, men would shovel snow into the covered bridges to form an ice pack so they could cross the span with their horse-drawn sleighs.

Both passenger and mail stagecoaches made daily trips outside the county to Cleveland, Warren, Youngstown and Erie.

Hotels, taverns, inns sprang up every ten miles on stage routes to accommodate travelers. The Jefferson Inn, located on the northeast corner of Jefferson and Chestnut streets, was built in 1826 by Quintus F. Atkin, a missionary to Indians and the first county sheriff.

The American House Hotel, founded in 1831, was built on the southwest corner of the same intersection. The Unionville Tavern survives as the best local remnant of stagecoach era fare and hospitality. Then, as now, the community's social life centered around socials and dances, which were often held at the local hotel.

The peddlers, or "tinkers," were commonplace, seen traveling from farm to farm with their wares and services. A shrewd breed of early salesmen, known for their inventiveness and for their colorful, cunning characters, the tinkers brought the tin kitchen, forerunner to modern cooking conveniences, to the Ohio frontier from New England.

Cont. Page 85

Caine Road Covered Bridge

Mechanicsville Road
Covered Bridge

Windsor Mills
Covered Bridge

Root Road
Covered Bridge

Previous page, Below & Next Page:

Sunset Lake Erie.

What fun to think
that there are Canadians
sitting on coastal park benches
looking South
wondering
if there are Americans
sitting on coastal park benches
looking North. How connected

Cont. from Page 78..

The first county fair was held in Austinburg in 1824 for the purpose of promoting agriculture, especially cheeses. A fifty-dollar cash award was given to the most improved farm in the area to stimulate innovation.

In 1825, the opening of the Erie Canal opened the Western Reserve to lakeshore access to eastern markets, and put pressure on Ohio legislators for an Ohio-Erie Canal connection. No canal was ever built in Ashtabula County, but the county was shaped by the Ohio canals built to the west and south – the Ohio Canal and the Cross-Cut Canal.

Water transportation of local goods was inexpensive, opened new markets for cheese, wheat, salt, whiskey and wood. The canals also brought the third migration to the Reserve – the Irish and German immigrants who provided the labor for their construction.

The first newspaper in Jefferson was "The Luminary," founded in 1828 with the purpose of serving anti-masonry interests. The short-lived "Ashtabula Recorder" was founded in 1823, "The Ashtabula Sentinel" in 1832, the same year Ashtabula County's first anti-slavery society was formed.

Prosperity had arrived in the county, but along with the prosperity and the leisure time it afforded came immense challenges of conscience. The settlers of the county were facing issues of local politics, the need for schools, the need for social services, of religion, and most importantly, of what stand to take on the national issues of slavery, states rights and expansion of the Union. Times were about to change, and the county would be in the middle and forefront of the issues which would bring on the Civil War.

***

Brown Memorial hospital originated in a home donated by W. H. Brown in 1919. It replaced Grace Hospital. The present building, now a part of University Hospital Health Systems, was constructed on the spot of the original home. Shown here are the new east entrance and the emergency entrance.

Ashtabula County Medical Center: Prior to the great train wreck of 1876, Ashtabula was served by doctors making house calls. During that catastrophic event, victims were cared for in private homes, promoting the citizens to form a committee for the establishment of a hospital. Ashtabula General Hospital started out in a small structure on June 20, 1904 at the present site. The main section of the present hospital was finished in 1952. On July 20, 1983, the name was changed to Ashtabula County Medical Center. A new addition, including a medical clinic, was opened in 1998.

There are so many ways to bridge

Above:

Harpersfield Covered Bridge.

Right:

South Denmark Rd. Covered Bridge.

Upper Right:

Creek Rd. Covered Bridge.

Lower Right:

Netcher Rd. Covered Bridge.

a

gap....

Brief, golden days of autumn
quiet the river,
creating opportunity for reflection,
preparing us
for the long, gray days that follow.

A North Kingsville pond south of Rt. 20.

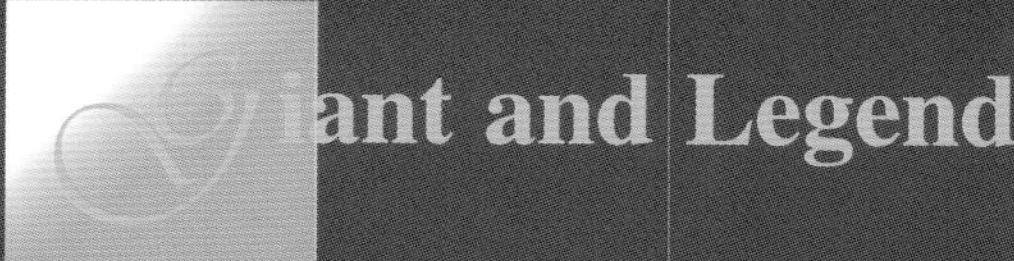iant and Legend

"Sooner than submit to such odious laws we will see the union dissolved; sooner than see slavery perpetuated we would see war; sooner than be slaves we will fight." Hartsgrove Township resolution in 1850.

The "ante-bellum" years in the young United States were full of debate, ambition, ideas of manifest destiny and troubled consciousness. No one person in the country did more to stir up the nation's moral consciousness than did Joshua Reed Giddings of Jefferson, Ohio.

For twenty-one years (1838-1859) he served as this district's representative in Washington, D. C., first as a Whig, then as a Free Soiler, and finally as a Republican. A staunch advocate of states' rights and an untiring advocate of anti-slavery, Giddings was known for his radical style of politics, and as a vigorous defender of human rights.

No northern political figure did more to channel opinion and move institutions against slavery. Using the "Ashtabula Sentinel" as his political mouthpiece, Giddings consistently followed his convictions and maintained personal integrity in lieu of choosing political expediency through compromise.

"The Sentinel" was edited by William C. Howells, the father of Jefferson resident William Dean Howells, the author who would become "America's foremost man of letters." The elder Howels Giddings' son Joseph Addison, and former editor Henry Fassett, remained faithful in reporting every opinion and act of legislator and agitator Giddings.

Giddings rarely missed the opportunity, on any issue before the house, to challenge his pro-slavery opponents on their motives for supporting expansion of the Union, for limiting free speech on the House floor, or for seeking war with Mexico.

Cascading apple blossoms invite deep breaths of imagined fragrance.

He believed the federal government should desist from permitting slave-trading and slave-holding in the District of Columbia because it supported the pro-slavery position against anti-slavery advocates. He believed federal troops should not be sent to Florida in the Seminole War because they really were there to recapture run-away slaves. He orated against the annexation of Texas and possible war with Mexico, because the nation's motive was to increase pro-slavery territory.

Giddings was the voice of America's consciousness in an age of pragmatic politics. He single-handedly was responsible for the repeal of the Atherton Gag Rule, which restored free speech and the right of petition to the floor of the House of Representatives.

Was he an abolitionist? Not until President Abraham Lincoln presented his Emancipation Proclamation. Giddings fought for abolition of slavery in Ohio and in the federal district in Washington, but until national emancipation was proclaimed the law of the land, he steadfastly upheld each state's right to determine its own destiny and policies.

Early in his political career, Giddings was a loyal Whig leader, who sought to align the party platform with the original ideals of the Declaration of Independence. He strived to unite all anti-slavery and moralist constituents by inclusion within the Whig Party. His political life was dedicated to a fusion of morality and conventional politics for the formation of a more humane society.

Abolitionists, especially in Ohio, didn't believe the Whigs went far enough in their anti-slavery beliefs. Thus, the Liberty and then the Free Soil parties were founded. Giddings eventually joined these more radical parties as he followed his conscience on the slavery issue. He never was able to reconcile his country's proclamation to the world of the virtues of freedom while it continued to practice and excuse slavery within its own borders.

Congressman Giddings was so huge a thorn in the sides of southern political pro-slavery Democrats that a Richmond, Virginia newspaper put a price on his head — $10,000 alive or $5,000 dead.

Perhaps his last major contribution to his country was his work on the platform for the new Republican Party in 1856. Here he was able to include in a political document language of the Declaration of Independence that "all men were created equal." Giddings is remembered as the "Champion of Freedom," and as "The Last of the Congressional Champions of Freedom."

The ever-agitating voice of Giddings and the actions of one man, who was to become the nation's greatest immortal legend – John Brown – did more to bring on the Civil War in its time and place in history than any other individuals in the country. Without their agitations, the nation was willing to blindly move to the future with compromise after compromise. These two men gave Ashtabula County the dubious distinction of precipitating the Civil War.

Above:

Sunset at Lake Erie, North Kingsville.

Previous Page:

A lone figure enjoys the peace and serenity of Lake Erie sunset at Lake Shore Park, Ashtabula

Next Page:

Fall beauty at Cederquist Park, Ashtabula.

To lose yourself
in a stand of trees
is to find
your
internal compass.

John Brown's invasion into Virginia with twenty-one men, and their subsequent raid on the federal arsenal at Harpers Ferry on Oct. 16, 1859, had its roots deep in Ashtabula County. He and his children emigrated earlier from Ohio to Kansas, seeking new land with the hope of keeping Kansas a free state. Weapons the Browns later used in the Kansas Border Wars were muskets shipped to the family by the Austinburg militia.

Bloody Kansas was no place to stay following Brown's execution of five pro-slavery settlers at Pottawatomie Creek and the ensuing Battle of Osawatomie. Brown returned to Ashtabula County and began planning his Virginia raid, which he was convinced would precipitate slave uprisings throughout the South similar to that of the 1831 Nat Turner Rebellion which left fifty-five whites dead.

John Brown spoke at the Congregational Church in Jefferson. Giddings passed the hat to help support the radical's activities. Two-hundred Sharps rifles and other weapons used in the raid were stored at the King and Brother's Cabinet Manufacturing Co. on Creek Road in Cherry Valley. Weapons were also hidden on the Alex Fobes' farm in Wayne Township. The majority of the members of his raiding party worked on farms in southern Ashtabula County.

Harpers Ferry, at the junction of the Potomac and Shenandoah rivers, was to fall under Confederate control three times during the war. The key Baltimore & Ohio railroad bridge was destroyed several times, and more than $1 million was spent during the war to rebuild and keep it open to rail traffic.

Secret organizations, the Black Strings and the Sons of Freedom, were formed within the county, members of which vowed to defend the life and property of any Ashtabula County man wanted as a witness or conspirator after the Harpers Ferry raid.

Locals vowed to disobey the Fugitive Slave Act requiring all citizens to assist in the apprehension and return of run-away slaves. There was debate on the Ohio House floor on whether Ohio should secede from the Union because of the issue. Giddings vocally supported both issues.

Jefferson at night. A fascinating combination of street and vehicle lights merge together

Adding to the growth of the John Brown legend was that Colonel Robert E. Lee led the federal forces at Harpers Ferry, which captured the Ohio raiding party. In the ranks of Lee's one-hundred troops were Jeb Stuart, Stonewall Jackson and John Wilkes Booth, all relative unknowns at the time, but each of whom was to make his mark in American history.

When John Brown was hung for treason in Charlestown, Virginia, he became a martyr for freedom, a rallying-point symbol for abolitionists and union soldiers alike for the duration of the War of Secession.

His raid and execution focused the attention of civilized citizens upon the evils of slavery in the United States. The day John Brown was hung, church bells tolled throughout Ashtabula County. That was the day the North took a stand on slavery and human rights, as northern women across the nation prayed for the man who gave his life so that millions of others might live free.

***

The War Years

"What sort of violence is that which is encouraged not by soldiers but by citizens, not so much by laymen as by ministers of the Gospel, not so much by fighting sects as by Quakers, and not so much by Quaker men as by Quaker women." Henry David Thoreau

The first Federal cannon fired in the War of Secession came from a Geneva company – Company F of First Regiment of Ohio Light Artillery.

Soon after, in 1861, Giddings called for volunteers for the 29th Ohio Volunteer Infantry, and mustered a roll of 1532, enough to form two companies, one from Jefferson and one from Pierpont. They trained at the county fairgrounds then known as Camp Giddings.

The 29th was to fight in 17 major battles, among them Chancelorsville, Gettysburg, Look-Out Mountain, Kenesaw Mountain, Sherman's March and Savannah. The flag of the 29th, made by local women, was later rescued from a Confederate prison and returned to action, and remains today on display in the Henderson Memorial Library in Jefferson.

Jefferson's Benjamin F. Wade, a former law partner of Joshua Giddings and later political enemy, was elected to the U.S. Senate in 1851. "Bluff" Ben Wade served for seventeen years as a fervent advocate of suffrage for blacks and equal rights for women.

The first man in the county to volunteer for Civil War duty, Wade was also known to keep a sawed-off shotgun in his Senate office desk for his personal protection. He became Lincoln's foremost critic on how the Union was fighting the war, referring to the early years as "Lincoln's Rose-Water War."

Wade was present as an observer at the first Battle of Bull Run in 1861. During the Rebel rout of Union troops, Wade was credited with rallying and reforming a regiment which helped prevent the Confederates from taking the capitol.

Through the duration of the war, Wade believed all southern traitors should be crushed and punished for their actions. This belief played a major role in the post-war impeachment proceedings of President Andrew Johnson as party members bolted Wade for Johnson, seeing the embattled incumbent president as the lesser of the two evils.

Had Wade's party remained consolidated behind his Senate leadership, Johnson would have been impeached and Wade would have become president. Instead, Johnson avoided impeachment by one vote.

His attitude of "total war" led directly to General George McClellan's removal by Lincoln as commander of the Union Armies, to General Ulysses S. Grant's rise in command, and to General T. Sherman's infamous March to the Sea.

As chairman of the Committee on Conduct of the War, Wade criticized Union political and military leaders for mismanagement of resources and for financial speculation in the South regarding the spoils of war.

Until the Union victories at Gettysburg and Vicksburg, the Confederates were winning the battles but couldn't gain foreign support to win the war. Wade's fearless and relentless pressure on Lincoln and his generals made much of the difference in both world opinion and on the front lines as Union forces mustered up to the task of preserving the union.

Cont. Page 108

Windy Hill golf course.

Conneaut's industrial area is highlighted by a Red Sunset maple as it contrasts with the stark white Foseco building nearby.

A seasonal water fall , Hogsback, Conneaut.

Known as a Rainbow Arch, this unique bridge is located on Mill Road just south of Conneaut City. It replaced a covered bridge in 1925.

Winter at Walnut Beach, Ashtabula.

"Winter wonderland" bests describes Ashtabula County's snowy season as depicted by this residential area in Conneaut.

Erie in January

The sun has gone south for the winter.
The lake's spirit is broken,
its summer-bright blue a murky brown.
Its high-spirited waves are tempered by
long, dark days,
arctic chill
and lowering sky,
vast gray lid that pushes down
—unforgiving—
rounding their tops,
stifling their play.
Exhausted by its struggle to resist,
the lake surrenders
and, like jello,
settles uncomfortably into

a new mold,
slowing
thickening
becoming heavy,
silent.
Whipped-frozen wave crests
await at the shore,
cream topping:
the only sweetness in January
on the north coast.
It's Erie.

Formations of ice and snow by
the public dock Conneaut.

Cont. from Page 100..

War plans prior to the Battle of Gettysburg were formulated in Ashtabula at the home of Peter H. Watson, who was serving as Assistant Secretary of War under Lincoln. Secretary of War Edwin M. Stanton, in Ashtabula for two weeks' rest, met with several Union generals to plan a great battle to end the war. The result was Gettysburg, previously known as "a dot on the map, where all roads crossed."

Ashtabula County's boast of "No fugitive slave can be taken from the soil of Ashtabula County back to slavery" proved good. The local "underground railroad" network shuttled hundreds of run-away slaves to freedom as they "followed the drinking gourd" enroute to the "land of the North Star" — Canada. Many remained in the Western Reserve to begin new lives as free citizens.

They avoided slave hunters, especially the Knights of the Golden Circle, a band formed in Richmond Township. This slave bounty-hunter organization, known as the Copperheads during the war, later became the Ku Klux Klan.

Fugitive slaves, often moving ever northward on their own or with the help of free Negroes and southern sympathizers, were alert for secret messages on quilts hanging on a clothesline which would lead them to a safe haven or secret hiding place. Often, the singing of a spiritual warned the run-aways to "get in the water, the dogs are comin'."

Many found sanctuary at the Carpenter and Kettunen houses in Andover Township, the Flack Store in Richmond Center, the Austin Ellsworth and Cowles homes in Austinburg, the Jefferson Inn (Station Anno Mundi) and the Jessie McDonald house in Jefferson, and finally at the Hubbard House (Mother Hubbard's Cupboard or Great Emporium) in Ashtabula Harbor, to name but a few of the dozens of safe-haven homes serving the Underground Railroad in the county.

The local abolitionist movement was fueled by Betsy Cowles, of Austinburg. Cowles formed the first women's anti-slavery society in the county, which soon boasted 224 members. Women wanted to be involved in the abolition movement, and when men resisted their efforts to become vocally active, the fairer sex gained insight into how the black Americans felt as second-class citizens.

Though Cowles wasn't aware of it at the time, her organizing of local women was the beginning of the women's equal rights movement in Ohio, which became the suffrage movement later in the 19th century. Cowles led equal rights conventions in both Salem, Ohio and at the Congregational Church in Jefferson. She worked side-by-side with former slave-abolitionist-woman's rights advocate Sojourner Truth.

Cowles, an 1840 graduate of Oberlin College and a school teacher for forty years, spoke out publicly on her beliefs: "Providence didn't open any doors for me; so I opened one for myself." She was especially vocal in support of civil rights for married women with property who paid taxes and had no vote.

An Ashtabula Bunker Hill native, Elizabeth Brown Stiles, lost her husband in the border wars of Bloody Kansas. She became a military nurse and traveled nineteen states with her thirteen-year-old daughter during the war, all the while serving as a spy for the Union army at President Lincoln's request.

Often in disguise with whitened hair, her granny cap and a pipe in her teeth, she would slip into enemy territory as an old southern woman seeking the wounded father of her granddaughter. Once arrested in Missouri, Stiles convinced General Price of the Confederate army that she was a Confederate spy with information from the North.

She once spent an entire night in a hogs' pen so she could eavesdrop on a Confederate officers' meeting which provided important and timely rebel troop movement information for Union generals. Later, captured a second time, she feigned illness for two weeks until she was able to escape and return to Union territory.

***

Growth and Prosperity

With the end of the Civil War also came the end of the frontier pioneer era in Ohio. Canals were outdated by the railroad. Mills fell into disrepair, giving way to foundries and "manufacturies."

The discovery of coal in southern Ohio, Kentucky and Virginia coupled with the discovery of iron ore in the upper Great Lakes region was to change the face of Ashtabula County, as well as the entire Midwest. Then oil was discovered in Titusville, Pennsylvania.

Steel began to be manufactured in Pittsburgh, Youngstown and then in Cleveland. Conneaut and Ashtabula harbors became key shipping points for raw materials. The north-south railroads connected the ore boats on the lakeshore with the foundries in the southern steel-making region.

The east-west railroad (The Great Atlantic to Pacific Railroad) connected the county to both eastern and western markets. Soon, floods of immigrants from Italy and Eastern Europe and Scandinavia arrived.

The Italians built the railroads and set up markets and warehouses for consumer goods and food products. The Eastern Europeans sought jobs in the mills, foundries and machine shops, while the Scandinavians worked in the shipyards in Ashtabula and Conneaut.

Prior to the post-war industrial period, Lake Erie played only a small role in Ashtabula County's development. The only navy battle ever fought on the lake was during the War of 1812 when Commodore Oliver Hazard Perry defeated two British warships – "The Queen Charlotte" and "The Detroit"—with the American ships, "The Lawrence" and "The Niagara," near Put-in-Bay.

Perry's famous words "We have met the enemy, and they are ours!" blazed across the headlines of Warren's "Trump of Fame" newspaper, announcing the end of the British threat to Ohio soil.

Lake Erie, however, has taken its toll during the years – more than 800 vessels lie on her bottom, victims of sudden storms and turbulent weather.

By the turn of the 20th century, the Great Lakes, and especially Lake Erie, were full of ore boats and paddleboat pleasure steamers. The success of the pleasure steamers was short lived. However, the shipyards of both Ashtabula and Conneaut were busy until the post-World War II era.

From the time Conneaut became the first iron ore dock on the Great Lakes, the port handled more Great Lakes tonnage than any lake port other than Chicago. The 1892 invention of the Hulett ore-unloader, by Conneaut resident George M. Hulett, revolutionized the shipping business. Ore boats could now be unloaded in a matter of hours by the "device with the huge clamshell jaws."

The 19th century "surplus farming" way of life in Ashtabula County gave way to the factories. The era in which farmers were kings and barns were palaces faded.

Margins blur
when one stands, grounded,
at the edge of the shore
and gazes
deep into the universe
where there are no limits.

Men worked for wages alongside strangers. The agrarian family way of life became a thing of the past as "interurban" streetcars closed distances between Jefferson, Ashtabula, Conneaut and Painesville.

The steam engine brought the true industrial revolution, providing regularity of production and opportunity for consolidation and monopoly. Steam's dependence upon fossil fuels brought prosperity to the area, along with a "pandora's box" of environmental and social challenges.

The creation of the State Bank of Ohio in 1845 also provided charters for a new class of independent banks which replaced earlier banks such as the Western Reserve Bank in Warren (1812) and the Commercial Bank of Lake Erie in Cleveland (1816). The Farmer's Bank in Ashtabula (1848) was one of those newly chartered by the state.

Ashtabula County, once known as the number-one shipper of dairy products in the nation to eastern and southern markets, was seeking a new identity. Ashtabula, for a few short decades, became known worldwide for its acres and acres of greenhouses, producing vegetables and flowers for world markets.

Geneva's native son, auto pioneer Ransom Eli Olds took his father's engine and created the Oldsmobile line of cars, while Ashtabula's Robert Morrison later became the first manufacturer of the all-plastic-bodied Corvette.

The New England style of architecture, manner of living and character of thinking remained beneath the surface of the county. But the migrations, first from Europe, then later from West Virginia and the Deep South, were to diversify and dilute the original "yankee flavor" of the area.

Even the industrial image of the county was to change, from shipbuilding to the chemical industries of the Cold War period. With the chemical industries came pollution of the county's streams and of Lake Erie.

Like the New England heritage of the Western Reserve, the land itself was to struggle for survival as the people who stayed here searched for a new identity with those who migrated here.

***

Left:
Sunset at Geneva-on-the-lake.

State Road Covered Bridge, with it's stunning fall colors, is a favorite during the Covered Bridge Festival held on the second weekend of October.

There are days
late in winter
when one must *believe in magic:*
spring will follow
a slow rumble through
an incomparable covered bridge.

Creek Road Covered Bridge, with it's rail fence and snow capped posts, stands out in contrast to the hazy winter background of white-coated tree branches.

One of our famous "lake effect" snows is evident
at this Parrish Road residence.

But no,
reality is deep on the other side
and patience is the lesson:
Spring comes to those who wait.

Each season
provides the opportunity
for trees to show themselves
differently.

How like us they are!
Standing alone
or standing among a crowd
they create a mosaic
that changes, itself,
each season.

Center Road bridge and lamp posts in fall overlooking CLYO, Skippon Park Center Road bridge offers a spectacular view of Conneaut Creek in all seasons. Built in 1990, it replaced an iron truss bridge and sets on the original sandstone abutments.

Left:

Railroad Museum, Conneaut

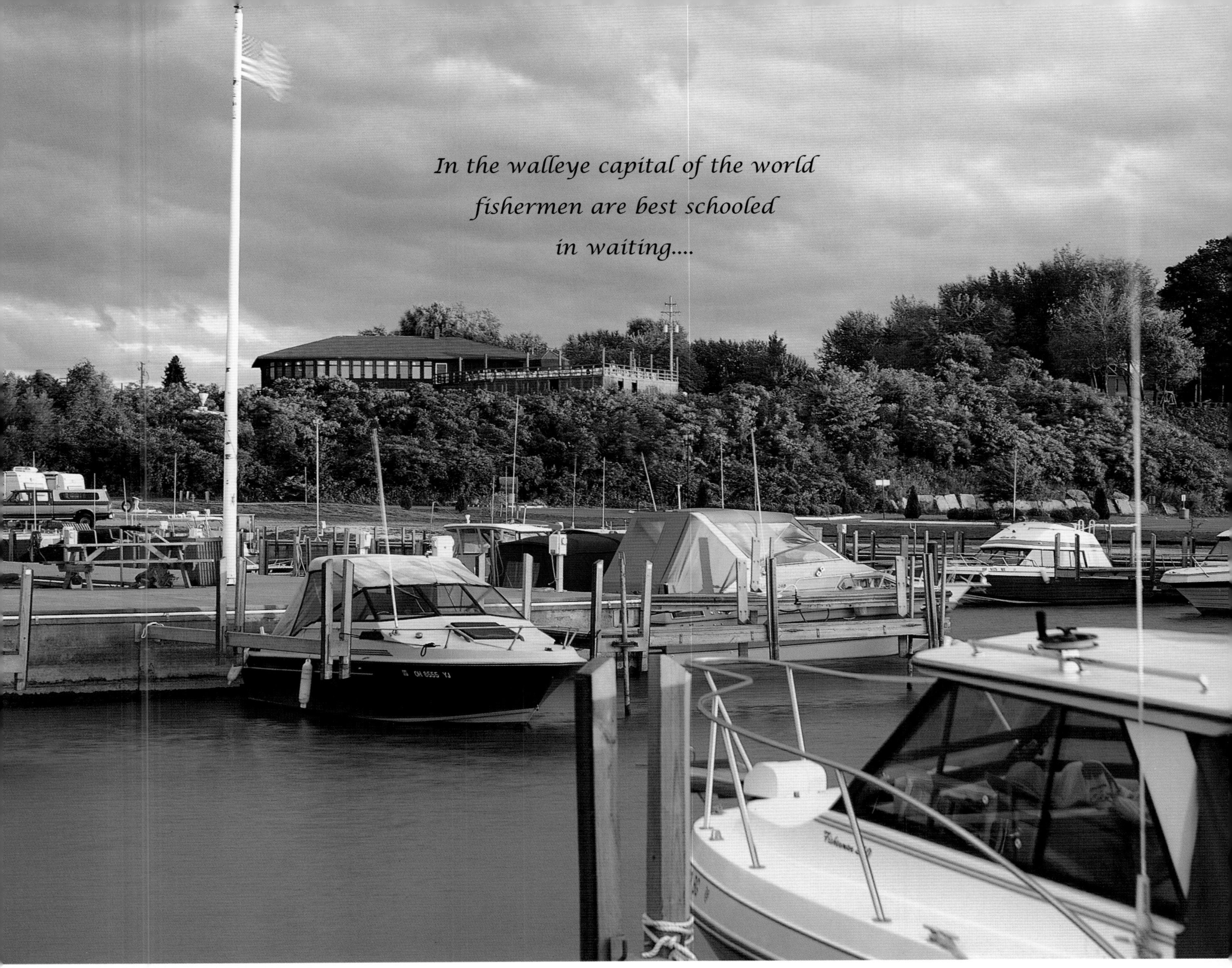
In the walleye capital of the world
fishermen are best schooled
in waiting....
OH 8555 YJ

The new home of the Loyal Order of the Moose Lodge, once a popular restaurant, overlooks the Public Dock in Conneaut.

JEFFERSON
OHIO

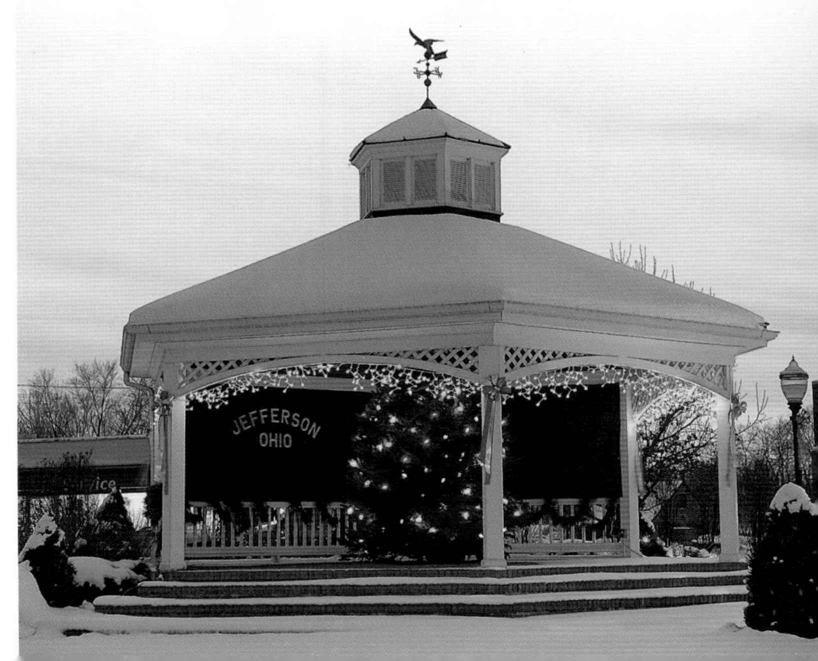

Christmas In Jefferson

The snow falls
silently,
with great respect,
covering loss.

Glenwood Cemetery across from Perkin's Restaurant in Conneaut.

Education

The first yankee pioneers from Connecticut were educated folk. During their early years in the Reserve, however, the settlers had a difficult time with the education of their children because there were no schools and all efforts of the pioneer families were needed for physical survival.

First log schoolhouses were built as small communities developed. One of the earliest schools was located in Bunker Hill at Jefferson Road in 1809. The first county classroom, 1804 in a Windsor blacksmith shop, grew to three schools by 1826, and served more than 100 students by 1835. By 1860, advanced courses were offered at the Orwell Academy and at the Grand River Institute.

Institutes sprung up in Burton, Kingsville and New Lyme. The Burton Institute was the forerunner to Western Reserve Institute in Hudson, which later became Western Reserve University in Cleveland.

The Jefferson Educational Institute, founded in 1844, when rebuilt in 1870 for $20,000, came complete with a Ladies' Boarding Hall. Tuition in 1901 was $12 per year for grades one through six; up to $24 per year for seniors. Boarding was available for twenty-five cents per week in the school hall or with a private family.

The Kingsville Institute, founded in 1835, became famous for the "Kingsville Experiment," the first concept in the nation for a centralized school system, the forerunner of consolidation. Included in the experiment was the concept of graded-school education for each and every child in the township. Education for all Ohio children became law in 1872.

The successful experiment resulted in the closing of small district, one-room schools, and the development of a state-paid transportation system. Horse-drawn "kid hacks" carried as many as twenty-five children per trip. Attendance problems disappeared and taxpayers saved money.

The Ashtabula Harbor Special School System, founded in 1879 to cope with the language barrier problem of the Finnish community, would be the final county district to consolidate when the high school joined Ashtabula High School in 2000 to form Lakeside High School.

New Lyme Institute, once known as the most beautiful campus in the state, fell victim to consolidation. Founded as a preparatory school (forerunner of today's junior colleges), the institute was known for its towered ediface, bells, wrought iron fences and mahogany woodwork.

The institute's most noted graduate was Florence E. Allen, the first woman to serve as an Ohio Supreme Court judge.

The two men who were to influence both local and national education were Geneva's Platt R. Spencer, the inventor of Spencerian writing, and Youngstown's William Holmes McGuffey, author of the McGuffey primers, spellers and readers. Both influenced generations of students with their educational innovations and philosophies.

***

Hardworking,
Ashtabula Countians create
mountains where none before existed,
and level them again
to fuel the Midwest.

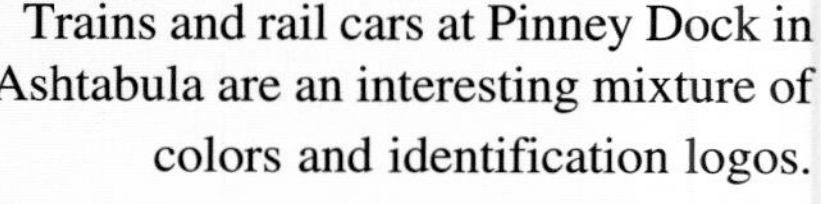

Trains and rail cars at Pinney Dock in Ashtabula are an interesting mixture of colors and identification logos.

Left:

Gazebo in North Park, Ashtabula.

Next Page:

The Christmas season is in full evidence around Ashtabula's municipal building.

Life and the Land

Besides the pollution of Lake Erie and its many feeder streams, the greatest impact man has had on the local landscape has been the draining of county swampland for development and the flooding of the Great Pymatuning Swamp.

The 17,000-acre swamp, previously a glacier-age lake, fed the United States troops in World War I, "providing everything for soup except the meat." The swamp farmers harvested tomatoes weighing two-to-three pounds, cauliflowers weighing fifteen pounds and cabbage the size of bushel baskets.

The rich, black mucky soil also provided a wealth of medicinal and healing plants, whose seeds were transplanted southward by the glacier. Once home and shelter to Indian tribes, the picturesque watery jungle of hardwoods was tangled with vines. Tree roots were entwined in knobby beds of moss near water pools covered with floating duckweed.

Home to poisonous plants, quicksand, and rattlesnakes, the swamp also bloomed with marsh marigolds, long-stemmed swamp violets, pink lady's slippers, rare yellow orchids, and pitcher plants. Royal and cinnamon ferns grew six feet tall.

Veterans Day Celebration,
Conneaut.

*Twenty-one guns
are not enough
to appropriately salute
those who have given
their lives
so that we might celebrate
the diversity
that is
Ashtabula County
...that is America.*

Ohio had little to say regarding the flooding of the swamp, as most of the lowland tract lay within Pennsylvania's borders. Seven thousand post-Depression jobs were created to clear the swamp, and in 1934, the Pymatuning Reservoir was dedicated as a marine paradise for fishing, boating and recreation. The reservoir became the water supply for surrounding communities as far away as Youngstown and Pittsburgh, while stabilizing the floodwaters of the Shenango and Beaver Rivers.

Ashtabula County remains unique in American history, and is often referred to as "Little Connecticut." Through the blending of six migrations and several emigrations, a sense of individualism remains.

The quieter way of life of yesteryear can still be found in the southern and central areas of the county. We'll have to search our memories, however, to see the menfolk harvesting ice on the lake, the children screaming on the wooden roller coaster at Woodland Beach Park to the accompaniment of the Big Bands playing in the nearby Casino Dance Hall, and the women tracing letters of the alphabet in the ashes before the hearth as they taught their children to read and write.

The revival of Lake Shore Park, which still sports the longest pavilion on the Great Lakes, and the cleaning of Fields Brook Creek bode well for the future. Plans for "greenway" trails and the continuation of Geneva-on-the-Lake's mile-long entertainment strip provide glimpses into the county's heritage and colorful past.

Century-old barns proclaim the up-coming bi-centennial celebration for Ohio and many local communities and counties. Underneath the newly painted advertisements remain yesterday's sales pitches for the May Company and for Mail Pouch Tobacco.

The morality, industry, adaptability, character and individuality of our county's residents remains intact, forever changing and evolving, from generation to generation, much the same as the peat bog evolves into a new forest, pond or field.

The magic of the land, woven with the mosaic of its inhabitants, is everywhere to see – especially for those who look at the present while seeing into the past.

***

Right:

Sunset ,
Lake Erie.

Myriad faces...
Nature's mosaic.

When we focus on the late-day sky,
a palette of colors washing the world
warm before us,
we connect to universal energy.

MARTHA STUMP BENSON: A "second time around" assisting Dr. Singh, Benson also helped with the compilation of "History of Ashtabula County" in 1985, co-authored "Conneaut High School, 100 Plus Years" in 1990, and is currently working on an upcoming series of books on Conneaut area history by Louise Passmore Legeza.

CLAUDIA GREENWOOD, PhD: is professor Emeritus of English at Kent State University, Ashtabula Campus. She continues to share her interest in poetry through a Poet's Circle at the Wellness & Total Learning Center, a poetry workshop for children with After School Discovery, and public readings. She and her husband, Bruce, live in Ashtabula.

FRANK OBERNYER: A native of Jefferson Township, received his B.A. from John Carroll University. He taught high school English and Drama at Cleveland Heights High School, and Physical Education at Colegio Bolivar in Cali, Colombia, prior to choosing a career as an entrepreneur businessman. Frank makes his home in Ashtabula County, has reported for the Star Beacon and Jefferson Gazette, and maintains his interests in writing, history, anthropology, theatre and photography.

Acknowledgments

Books don't just happen. The process of producing one will never cease to amaze me. That said, I wish to thank everyone who helped make this one possible, because it was by no means a solo effort.

I express special thanks to Frank Obernyer, Claudia Greenwood and Martha Benson for their hours of work and special talents for the making of this book.

Thanks to Frank for his hours of dedicated research into the heritage and history of our county. His story-telling gifts bring the photographs alive with a depth and understanding of the dreams and lives of our ancestors.

Thanks to Claudia for her beautiful and invaluable poetry. She has given great insight into the photographs in this book and inspiration to the beauty of Ashtabula County.

Thanks to Martha for her talents with text and history. Her dedication to my projects is very much appreciated.

I want to express a very special thanks to my family and friends who never stopped giving me encouragement for the making of another book. My wife and children were especially supportive and patient with my photography work.And last but not the least my sincere thanks to Jasneet Devgun,Chiranjeev Devgun and Jaspreet Devgun for their expert ideas of artistic graphics.

Thanks to my family; Gurjit, Puneet, Jasneet for their sincere support and patience.